PUFFI

WINGS A
How an Aircraft Flies

Have you ever wondered just how a jumbo jet, with its vast bulk and weight, even gets off the ground, let alone flies huge distances at high speed? If so, this book will show you how it's done.

Not only does the author explain clearly how an aircraft flies, but he also describes simple activities that anyone can do to demonstrate just what happens: make a simple wing out of cardboard, and see for yourself how it works; use a hair-drier to see the effect of an aircraft engine; and see how a rudder and elevators affect the flight of a paper dart.

Using readily available, inexpensive items, these activities vividly illustrate the basic scientific principles underlying one of the major technological advances of the twentieth century. Written and illustrated in a lively, friendly style, this innovative book is an ideal starting place for anyone wanting to know how aircraft fly.

Neil Ardley, winner of the 1989 Science Book Prize, is the author of many books for children on science subjects. Being a keen musician and composer, he has also written for children on music. He divides his time between homes in London and Derbyshire.

Also by Neil Ardley

Snap Happy – how a camera takes pictures
Tune In – how TV and radio work
Bits and Chips – how a computer works

Neil Ardley

WINGS AND THINGS

How an Aircraft Flies

Illustrated by
David Woodroffe

PUFFIN BOOKS

Consultant: Andrew Nahum, Curator of
Aviation, The Science Museum, London

PUFFIN BOOKS

Published by the Penguin Group
27 Wrights Lane, London W8 5TZ, England
Viking Penguin, a division of Penguin Books USA Inc.,
375 Hudson Street, New York, New York 10014, USA
Penguin Books Australia Ltd, Ringwood, Victoria, Australia
Penguin Books Canada Ltd, 2801 John Street, Markham,
Ontario, Canada L3R 1B4
Penguin Books (NZ) Ltd, 182–190 Wairau Road, Auckland 10,
New Zealand

Penguin Books Ltd, Registered Offices: Harmondsworth,
Middlesex, England

First published 1990
10 9 8 7 6 5 4 3 2 1

Printed in England by Clays Ltd, St Ives plc
Filmset in Melior

CONTENTS

CHAPTER 1
GETTING A LIFT

FLAP

FLAP

Being able to fly, birds can go anywhere. Obstacles like rivers, forests, mountains and even seas mean nothing to them: some birds can fly from one end of the world to the other. They can fly fast too. Even record-breaking athletes are easily outpaced by the fastest of birds. It's no wonder then that when people first thought of taking to the air, they tried to fly like birds.

Through the ages, bird-men have often attempted to heave themselves into the air. They strapped home-made wings to their arms and bravely threw themselves from high places. But no matter how hard they flapped their arms, they simply could not fly. Sensible bird-men launched themselves over water and knew how to swim. Then the crash landing that always followed was wet but safe.

So why can birds fly but we cannot? And not just birds but bats, butterflies and balloons as well as airliners and helicopters – what keeps all of them up in the air? The answer is lift, so let's find out about lift. It's rather like the lift that carries us from one floor to another in a big store.

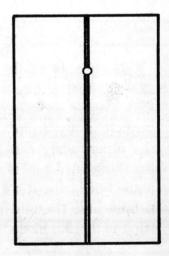

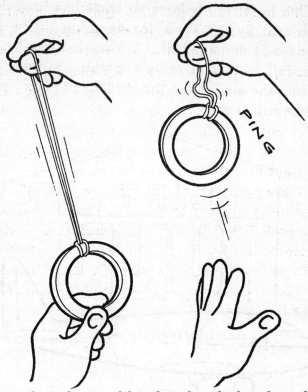

Take a long rubber band or link a few short bands together. Loop one end around a reel of sticky tape (you're going to need some later on) and suspend the reel from one hand. Pull the reel down with the other hand and let go. It flies up into the air, pulled by the stretched rubber bands. Stretch the bands more, and they pull the reel more strongly so that it flies higher. Be careful not to hurt yourself or anyone else doing this.

This is fairly obvious, so what has it to do with real flying? Well, for anything to fly, it needs a force called lift. A force is a push or pull. Lift pushes or pulls something to raise it up into the air, just as the stretched bands pull up the reel of tape.

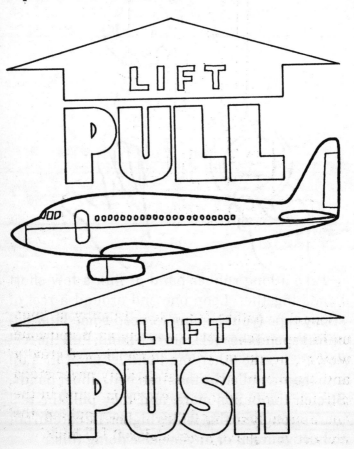

There's another force too. Usually it pins us to the ground just as surely as if someone were sitting on us. It's called the force of gravity and it gives us our weight. Gravity never stops pulling – even when something is flying in the air. The rubber bands soon stop pulling the reel and it is gravity that makes it fall back.

If we are to fly, lift must overcome our weight, not only to raise us up into the air but to keep us there. A bird produces lift with its wings. The lifting force easily overcomes its weight because a bird is very light, and it soars aloft as if hauled up by an invisible string. The bird-men crashed to earth because people are just too heavy to fly under their own power. The lift of their flapping wings was nowhere near strong enough to overcome the force of gravity pulling them down to the ground. Gravity always wins this uneven contest.

We therefore need another way of producing a powerful lift in order to fly. Flying machines do this in several ways to carry us up into the air.

CHAPTER 2
FLYING BY FLOATING

There's a very simple way of producing lift to make things fly. It could be going on around you right now, but it's totally invisible. However, you can show this kind of lift in action. A hot radiator is needed so if the weather is warm you must ask someone to switch the heating on. Wait until the radiator is hot.

Take a short length of stiff wire and bend it into a loop. Put some washing-up liquid into a cup and dip the loop in it. A film forms across the loop as you take it out. Blow gently into the loop and you'll get a stream of bubbles. Now

blow some bubbles over the radiator. As the bubbles pass over the radiator, some will suddenly shoot up into the air. Some may even reach the ceiling.

HOTTING UP

The bubbles get a lift because hot air rises. The radiator heats the air around it and this air rises above the radiator, carrying the bubbles upwards with it. The reason for this is that hot air is lighter than cool air. Light things rise to float on heavier materials, just as wood floats on water. Hot air gives us a way of flying by floating in the air, and this is how a hot-air balloon works.

People have seen this happening for thousands of years. It's why smoke travels upwards above a fire and collects to float high in the air. But it was only two centuries ago that someone thought of using hot air to fly. In 1783, the first hot-air balloon took to the air in France carrying the Montgolfier brothers aloft.

THE MONTGOLFIERS'
HOT-AIR BALLOON

Just like hot-air balloons today, this balloon carried its own fire to heat the air. Hot-air balloons have a gas burner fixed to the basket beneath the huge balloon. Air heated by the hot flames from the burner rises and collects in the balloon. When the air inside the balloon is hot, it gives enough lift to overcome the balloon's weight. The balloon rises from the ground and soars up into the sky, carrying one or two people in the basket.

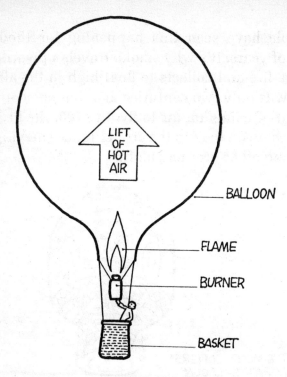

LIFT
OF
HOT
AIR

BALLOON

FLAME

BURNER

BASKET

As it rises, the hot air in the balloon begins to cool and the lift gets weaker. When the lift equals the balloon's weight, the balloon stops rising and floats at the same height in the air. Then, as the hot air cools some more, the lift becomes less than the balloon's weight and this weight begins to pull the balloon down. To keep the balloon flying, the people turn the burner on again. Short bursts of flame keep the air inside hot. The lift stays strong enough to keep the balloon flying.

16

GAS BAG

Hot air is not the only way to keep a balloon aloft. Filling the balloon with a gas that is lighter than air can also give it enough lift to make it fly. The balloons that fly highest of all are gas balloons. Hydrogen is the lightest gas. It's used to fill the small balloons that fly long distances in competitions.

However, hydrogen can catch fire and is dangerous. So the balloons sold by street vendors contain helium, a light gas that is safe. Such a balloon floats on the end of a long string, and it will show you how a balloon can fly.

Do this inside a room, otherwise you'll need to train some homing pigeons to fetch your balloon back. Tie some more string or a piece of card to the balloon's string. You'll need enough to make the balloon heavier than its lift so that it sinks to the floor. Now cut off small pieces of the string or card to make the balloon lighter. You'll reach a point where the balloon just floats. The balloon's lift is now equal to its weight. Cut off a bit more string or card so that the weight just becomes less than the lift, and the balloon will slowly rise. Take care using scissors.

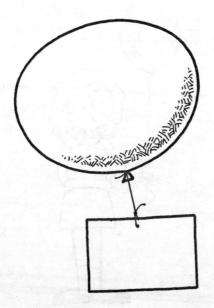

SHIPS IN THE SKY

It's a good idea to look at the weather forecast before flying in a balloon. Sunshine makes a flight pleasant, but it's more important to find out about the wind. It's the wind that pushes the balloon through the air from place to place. So, to get somewhere, you've got to make sure that the wind is blowing in the right direction.

Balloons are therefore quite useless as a form of transport to fly from one place to another. You could wait days for the wind to blow in the right direction. Even then, it might stop or change direction once you are airborne. To fly to a particular place, a balloon needs an engine to power it in the air.

BALLOON RACE
THIS WAY

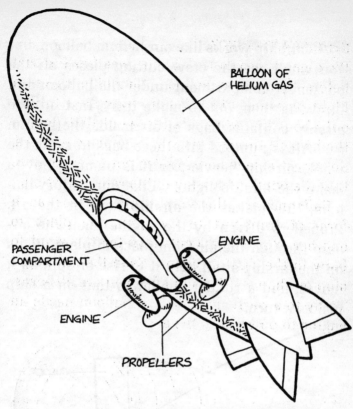

BALLOON OF HELIUM GAS

PASSENGER COMPARTMENT

ENGINE

ENGINE

PROPELLERS

An ordinary balloon can only carry a few people up into the sky. An engine is much too heavy for it. A powered balloon has to produce much more lift in order to carry an engine as well as passengers. Such a balloon is called an airship. It usually contains helium gas, which has more lifting power than hot air. Even so, the airship has to be huge to fly. It really is like a ship floating in the sky instead of on water.

An airship works like our helium balloon, but you won't see the crew cutting pieces off the passenger compartment under the balloon and throwing them out to make it fly! Instead, the airship contains bags of air inside the helium gas. Air is pumped into these bags to make the whole airship heavier, or it is pumped out to make the airship lighter. Like our helium balloon, this makes the airship float in the air. Propellers driven by the engine push the airship through the air from place to place. Flaps on the airship's tail help it to rise or sink as it moves, and a rudder similar to that on a ship makes it turn.

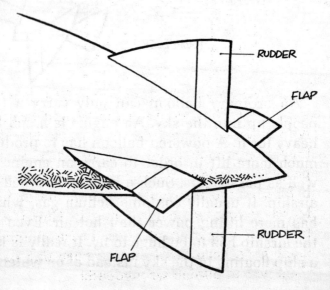

RUDDER

FLAP

RUDDER

FLAP

CHAPTER 3
AIR ON THE MOVE

Who do you think were the first people to fly? They were not the Wright brothers, who invented the aeroplane in 1903. Nor were they the French balloonists of 1783. In fact, people first flew at least five hundred years before. In the thirteenth century, the explorer Marco Polo saw people flying in China. They took to the air in giant kites. These kite flights must have been terrifying because one use of them was to punish wrongdoers!

Kites come in many different shapes and sizes. Here's a kite that is very easy to make and which flies well. Take a plastic bag like a pedal-bin liner. Cut it open to make the shape shown and tape two wooden sticks to it. Then attach a piece of string to the corners. Next, wind a long length of string on to a cardboard tube and tie it to the piece on the kite.

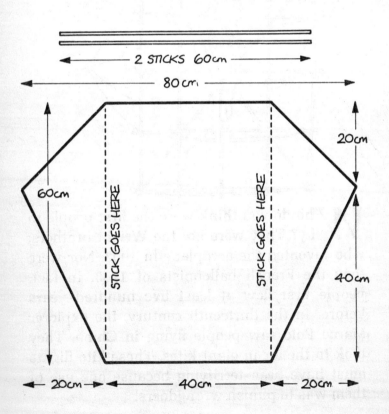

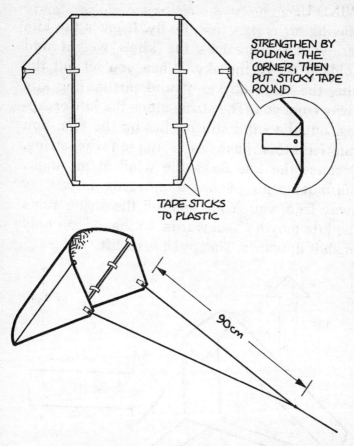

STRENGTHEN BY FOLDING THE CORNER, THEN PUT STICKY TAPE ROUND

TAPE STICKS TO PLASTIC

90cm

The kite is now ready to fly. Let it out on the string in a brisk wind and it will rise up into the sky. Jerk the string and the kite will swoop. If the wind drops, so will the kite. But you can make it rise by pulling in some string or by running to pull the kite through the air.

WIND UP

Moving air makes the kite fly. It gives the kite lift, which overcomes the kite's weight and holds it up in the sky. When you let out the kite, the wind strikes it and pushes the kite away from you. The string stops the kite escaping, but the wind still pushes on the kite. You can feel this push as a tug on the string. Because the kite faces the wind at an angle, the moving air pushes it upwards as well as away from you. Your hold on the string stops the kite moving backwards, so the air can only push it upwards. This push is its lift.

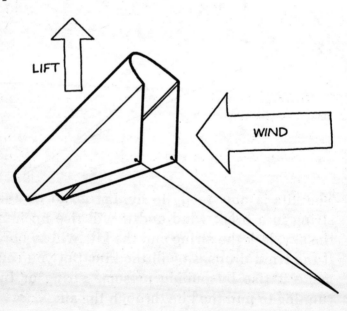

LIFT

WIND

As you let out the string, the kite rises. Don't let the string out too quickly as the kite will be pushed back and will lose lift. In a strong wind, the kite will get lots of lift and fly high. When it is flying steadily, you are also pulling down on the string and preventing the lift from pushing it higher in the sky. Pulling the kite forwards increases the speed at which air meets the kite. This makes lift stronger and the kite rises. Pulling, releasing and jerking the string changes lift so that you can control the flight.

PRESSURE POWER

Moving air makes many other kinds of things fly, and we're going to make it fly a ping-pong ball. You'll need a vacuum cleaner that can blow air out through its pipe instead of sucking air in. Ask an adult to set up the cleaner for you and switch it on. If your vacuum cleaner does not blow, a hair-drier might work instead.

Point the pipe or drier so that the air blows upwards. Now place the ping-pong ball in the stream of moving air. The ball should hover above the pipe or drier. That's not too surprising as the moving air is holding up the ball. But now tilt the pipe or drier. The ball moves to one side and is suspended in mid-air!

● If you are using a hair-drier, switch it to cool or cold if possible so as to avoid heating anything.

The reason for this amazing result is air pressure. Air has a certain pressure. This means that the air presses on any surface it meets. The air around you presses strongly on your body, for example. If you breathe out as much air as you can, you'll see (and feel) the air pressure pushing in your stomach and chest.

AIR PRESSURE

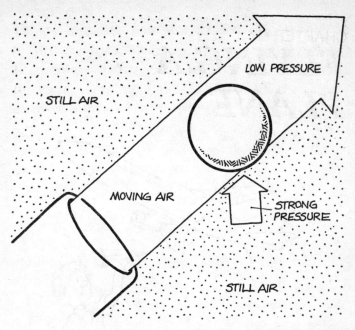

When air moves, its pressure weakens. The stream of moving air that comes from the pipe of the vacuum cleaner or from the hair-drier has a lower pressure than the still air around it. When the ping-pong ball begins to move outside the stream, the strong pressure of the surrounding air pushes it back into the stream and keeps it there. The force of the moving air stops the ball falling down and it hovers in the air stream.

This power of moving air is very important in aircraft, and makes gliders, planes and helicopters fly.

CHAPTER 4
FLYING A PLANE

*F*ew people get to fly in balloons or airships, or take to the air beneath a giant kite. Almost all of us fly in airliners, which are passenger aircraft with wings. An aircraft that flies with wings is called an aeroplane or airplane, or just a plane for short.

WINGS FOR FLIGHT

How can wings hold a plane up in the air? The answer is lift, which the wings produce as they cut through the air. Lift gets more powerful as a plane travels forwards faster. This is why a plane has to rush along a runway to take off. Only in this way can the wings produce enough lift to overcome the plane's weight and rise into the air. An aircraft like a jumbo jet with its hundreds of passengers is very heavy. It has to take off at high speed for the wings to produce enough lift.

Let's show a wing in action. To do this, it's easier to keep the wing still and blow air around it. This is the same as having the wing move through the air. Make a wing with a sheet of paper that is fairly stiff. Firmly fold the sheet on a line slightly off centre. Then use sticky tape to fasten the edges together so that the larger half curves upwards.

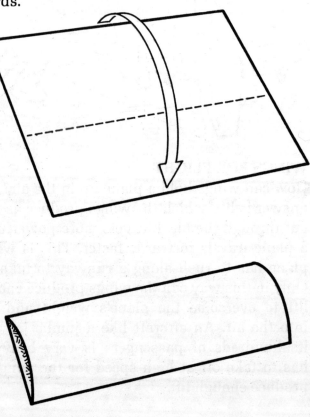

Make small holes in the top and bottom of the centre of the wing and put a short piece of a straw through it as shown. The straw must fit tightly into the wing. Next, thread some cotton through the straw. Then place a chair or stool on its side and fasten the cotton to two of the legs. The wing should be free to move up and down the cotton, which must be taut.

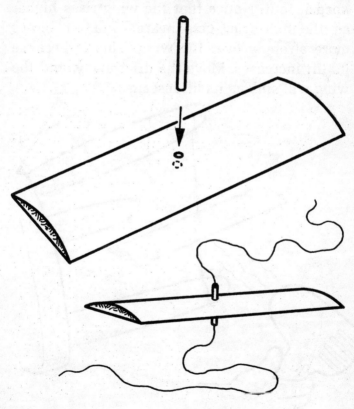

Use a hair-drier to blow air over the wing. Handle the hair-drier with great care as it may get hot. Hold the hair-drier some way from the wing, and switch on. Turn the wing if necessary so that it stays facing the hair-drier. Now slowly bring the hair-drier towards the wing. It should rise up the cotton and begin to fly! It may help to press a finger against the cotton to keep it taut. Notice that the wing rises higher as the hair-drier gets nearer and air blows more strongly over the wing. This is because its lift increases. Move the drier away, and the wing will sink as its lift lessens.

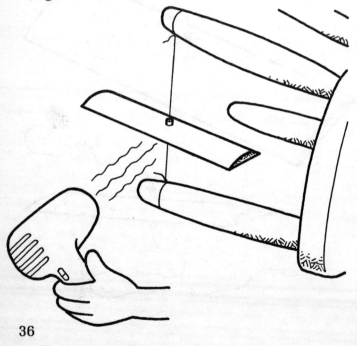

Sometimes, the wing may flutter as the lift changes slightly. This happens in a plane, and you can see the wings bend slightly as it flies.

DARTING THROUGH THE AIR

Wings fly because of their shape. The top of a wing is curved and underneath it is almost flat. This shape is called an aerofoil or airfoil.

A wing parts the air as it moves. Air that is struck by the top of the wing has to move up and then down as the wing passes. The wing deflects the air and makes it move faster, so its pressure weakens. But air underneath the wing hardly moves at all. The stronger pressure of the still air under the wing pushes the wing upwards. In this way, the wing produces lift.

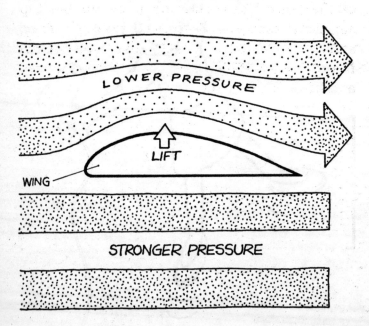

LOWER PRESSURE

LIFT

WING

STRONGER PRESSURE

To see how a plane flies, let's make one. A paper dart is quick and easy, and it looks and flies rather like the super-fast airliner Concorde.

Take a sheet of A4 paper and fold it down the centre. Then fold the corners and sides into the centre as shown. Fold one side back, then turn the paper over and fold the other side back. This is your basic dart, but it needs a little more work. Fold the point back into the dart and fold up two fins along the sides of the wings. Fix two or three paper clips to the back of the base. Then carefully push up the top surface of each wing to curve it slightly into an aerofoil. Hold the dart by its base and launch it into the air. It should fly before losing speed and lift to land – or crash!

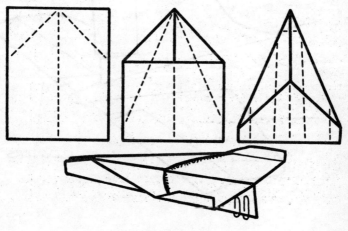

AT THE CONTROLS

As well as lifting itself into the sky, a plane also has to use the air to turn and to climb and dive. For this reason, a plane has a tail as well as wings. Most planes have a separate tail at the back. It has a vertical fin and a horizontal stabilizer like two small wings. On the fin is a rudder, and the stabilizer has two elevators. The pilot controls these to fly the plane. They swivel out into the air as the plane moves, and the air pushes them to make the plane change direction.

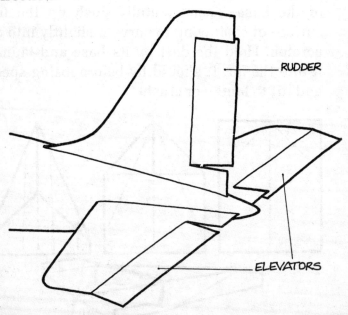

RUDDER

ELEVATORS

Like Concorde, our dart does not have a separate tail, but we can use it to show how a pilot controls a plane. Make a small cut in the back end of the base to form a rudder. Bend it and fly the dart a short distance. See how turning the rudder makes the dart turn in the same direction.

Make elevators with small cuts at the back of the dart's wings. Turn them up and fly the dart a short way. See how the elevators make the nose of the dart rise so that it begins to climb. Turning them down makes the dart dive. Always take care flying the dart.

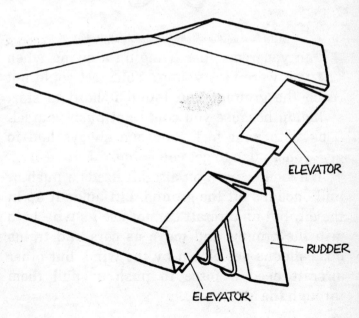

ELEVATOR

RUDDER

ELEVATOR

CHAPTER **5**

PUSH AND PULL

*C*an you remember being on a swing when you were very young? Your feet could not reach the ground. You found it hard to start swinging because you could not push yourself back with your feet. Someone always had to give you a push to get you going.

In a similar way, an aircraft needs a push or pull once it's off the ground. Lift holds it up in the air, but an aircraft cannot use its wheels to grip the ground and move as cars and trains do. Balloons get blown by the wind, but other aircraft need a force to push or pull them through the air.

GLIDERS AND GRAVITY

A glider uses the pull of gravity to move forwards through the air. A big glider is first hauled up into the air on a cable. Then the pilot releases the cable. A hang-glider can simply run down a slope into the wind to get airborne. The glider then begins to fall but flies on, supported by the lift of its wings. It slowly sinks, as if it were slipping down a long invisible slide in the sky.

A glider can get more lift by finding rising streams of air. These then carry the glider back up into the sky just as, in Chapter 2, the rising warm air above a radiator lifted bubbles.

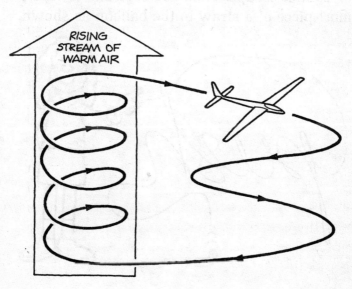

RISING STREAM OF WARM AIR

BLOWING ALONG

Gliders are fine for sport. But they are useless as a means of transport as they cannot do much more than search for rising air, perhaps without success. To fly from one place to another at high speed, an aircraft needs something to give it a powerful push. It gets this push from the air itself!

A simple balloon will show you how this happens. Blow one up and let it go, and it will fly around the room. A better way is to make the balloon fly along a long piece of cotton or thin string stretched across a room. Blow up the balloon and hold it by the neck so that the air cannot escape. Then ask someone to tape a short piece of a straw to the balloon as shown.

Thread the cotton or string through the straw. Hold the cotton or string tight and release the neck of the balloon. It flies off at high speed.

The balloon moves as the air escapes from the neck. The air comes out backwards and the balloon moves forwards. The escaping air pushes on the balloon.

POWER IN THE AIR

An aircraft has engines to make the air move. It has either propellers or jet engines. We can use a hair-drier to show how they work. Take care doing this as a hair-drier uses electricity and may get hot. It is best to ask an adult to help you so that you do not hurt yourself or anyone else.

Clear a large area on a hard floor (not carpeted) and lay a line of colouring pens or pencils on it as shown. Cover the pens or pencils with a piece of card big enough for the hair-drier to rest on. The area must be near a power point with a switch. Make sure that the power point is switched OFF. Then plug in the hair-drier. Move the drier switch to ON. The drier will not start because the power is off.

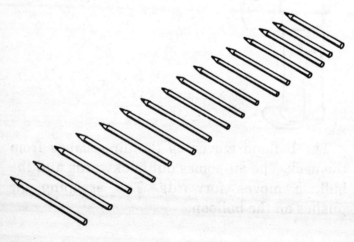

Lay the drier on the card as shown, attaching it loosely with sticky tape. Make sure the wire is loose. Now switch on the power point. The hair-drier starts and moves along the line of pens. Switch off before the drier hits anything.

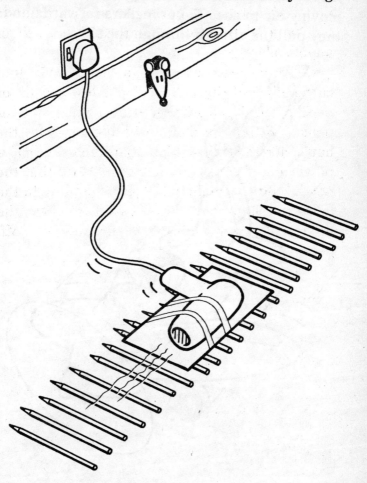

Inside the hair-drier is a fan. It spins round to drive air out of the drier. As the air leaves, it pushes the hair-drier so that it rolls along the pens. The propellers on an aircraft spin to move air backwards in the same way. The moving air pushes the propellers forwards and they pull the aircraft through the sky.

JETS FOR SPEED

Fast aircraft have jet engines. These engines look like big hair-driers fixed under the wings. In fact, jet engines are similar inside. A fan spins to move air through the engine. The air is heated and a jet of hot air comes out of the back of the engine.

However, jet engines make the air very hot with flames of burning fuel. As the hot air comes out of the jet engine it moves very fast, pushing the engine and the aircraft forwards with great power. This happens because air expands when it gets hot and so rushes out of the back of the jet engine at high speed.

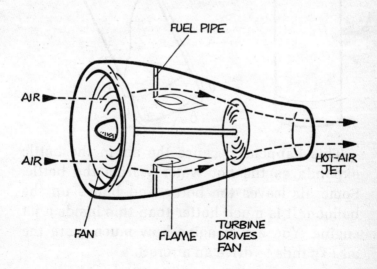

FUEL PIPE

AIR

AIR

HOT-AIR JET

FAN   FLAME   TURBINE DRIVES FAN

You can show how heating air makes it expand with an empty plastic bottle and a balloon. Fit the mouth of the balloon tightly over the open top of the bottle. Now place the bottle in the sink. Turn on the hot tap so that hot water runs over the bottle. The balloon will begin to fill, standing up and swelling in size.

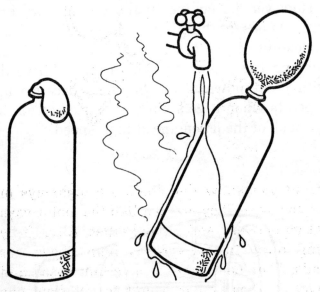

This happens because the air in the bottle expands as the hot water warms the bottle. Some air leaves the bottle and blows up the balloon. It is much hotter than this inside a jet engine. You can imagine how much more the air expands to drive an aircraft.

CHAPTER 6
HIGHWAYS IN THE SKY

Did you know that there are highways in the sky? They are just like the motorways that go between and around cities. Aircraft fly along these invisible roads high above our heads. They have to go at a certain speed and travel at a particular height to get from one place to another.

Pilots use these highways, or flight lanes, for safety. Aircraft fly so fast that a collision could destroy them. By keeping to the flight lanes, which are all one-way only, aircraft never come near each other.

There are no police in the air to make sure that pilots behave. However, people on the ground are watching them. These people are air-traffic controllers. They know where all the aircraft are in their regions of the sky. The controllers use radar to watch the aircraft.

SAFETY SIGNALS

You can easily show how radar works. You need to do this in a place with an echo. Stand in front of a high wall or cliff, or a long tunnel or building with an echo. Clap your hands sharply and you will hear the sound come back a little later. This is the echo. Walk towards the echo and clap again. The echo returns sooner. Walk away and the echo takes longer.

CLAP

You hear the echo because the sound made by your hands travels through the air to the wall. The sound bounces off and comes back to your ears so that you hear it again. The length of time of the echo depends on how far you are from the wall. An echo from a distant wall takes longer because the sound travels further.

Radar works in the same way. Instead of sound, it uses invisible rays. The rays come from a big radar aerial at an airport. The rays travel a million times faster than sound. They rush through the air and strike aircraft. The rays bounce off and travel back to the aerial in a fraction of a second.

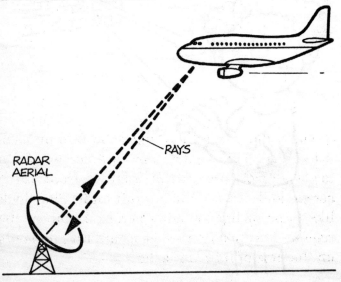

RAYS

RADAR
AERIAL

The radar turns the radar echo into an electric signal. This signal goes to a screen like a television set. The controller sits in front of the screen and can see the aircraft on it. They look like blips of light moving across a map of the region. The position of each aircraft depends on the time of its radar echo.

Each aircraft also sends its own radar signal to the radar aerial. The signal tells the radar how high the aircraft is flying. It also gives the flight number of the aircraft. This information appears on the screen. In this way, the controller can see where all the aircraft are and knows which aircraft is which.

TALL TALK

The controller has to direct each pilot. The pilot knows where the aircraft is going, but he or she does not know where all the other aircraft are flying. So the controller talks to the pilot by radio. The controller instructs each pilot and tells them where to fly by giving them their height, speed and direction. The controller makes sure that none of the aircraft will come near each other as they speed through the air.

The controller also has to direct aircraft to land at an airport. Sometimes several aircraft arrive at the same time. The controller tells the pilots to fly in circles around the airport. Then each aircraft has to wait for its turn to land.

You can play a game to find out how the controller keeps aircraft flying safely through the air. Play outside where there are no obstacles to hurt people. One person is the controller at an airport and the others are aircraft. Each aircraft has its own flight number, like BA123. The letters show which airline the

aircraft belongs to; BA is British Airways. The controller stands in the middle and all the aircraft come in to land by the controller at the same time. The controller has to direct all the aircraft. Use the flight numbers, and say how fast and how far away each aircraft must fly and when and where to turn. Each aircraft must follow the controller's directions exactly, and no one should look round to watch the other aircraft.

If a collision is about to happen, stop the game. Choose a new controller and start again. The winner is the first person to get all the aircraft to land safely.

AIRCRAFT RADAR

Aircraft also use radar to find out how high they are in the air. A radar set on the aircraft sends radar rays down to the ground or sea below. The rays bounce off the surface and return to the aircraft. The time of this echo depends on how high the aircraft is above the ground or sea. The radar turns the echo into an electric signal which goes to the pilot's height indicator.

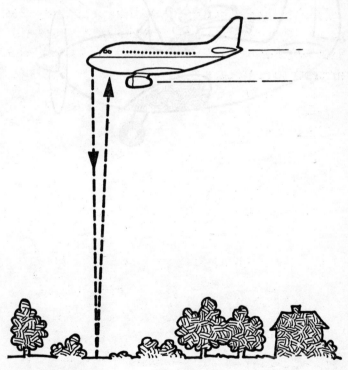

Aircraft also use radar to find out about storms a long way ahead. The radar rays bounce off raindrops in the storm. If the radar warns the pilot of a storm, the aircraft can change course to fly around it.

CHAPTER 7
FINDING THE WAY

WHICH WAY TO WALES?

An airliner flying out over an ocean or a remote region like a desert is on its own. There are no controllers below to help guide the pilot through the sky to a distant airport. The airliner may fly thousands of kilometres and on the way winds may try to blow it off course. Yet the aircraft stays on course and arrives at the airport.

How does the airliner find its way? There's nothing to see below that could give the pilot any clue to its whereabouts. In fact, computers on the airliner are able to keep it on course. As it flies through the air, the computers work out the position of the airliner on the earth's surface. They check that this position is on the way to the airport.

ON THE SPOT
A map of the world has sets of lines on it. These are not actual lines that cross the land and sea. They are lines that mark positions on the earth's surface. Every position on the earth has two numbers and letters. These are called its latitude and longitude. The lines have numbers that give the latitude and longitude.

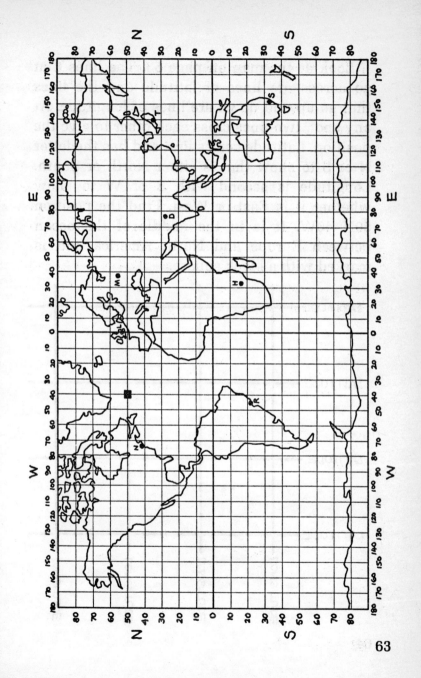

63

Look at the map on page 63. The lines that go across are lines of latitude and the lines that go up and down are lines of longitude. At any spot, two lines cross each other to give the position. Latitude comes first and has the letter N or S to show that is either North or South. Longitude is second with E or W to show whether it is East or West. Find the position 50N 40W. It is in the middle of the ocean between Europe and North America and is marked with a black square.

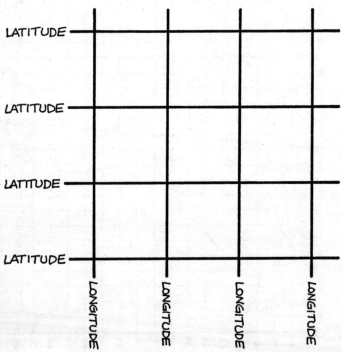

The letters on the map show the positions of several cities. They are:

D   Delhi, India
H   Harare, Zimbabwe
L   London, UK
M   Moscow, USSR
N   New York, USA
R   Rio de Janeiro, Brazil
S   Sydney, Australia
T   Tokyo, Japan

WELCOME TO 40 N 116 E

FLIGHT PLAN

Two people can play a game with this map. Make two photocopies of it, one for each player. You must imagine that you each have an airline with airliners flying between the cities. Using pencils, both players first mark the positions of three airliners. Use a small square to mark each position and fill in the square. A flight from London to New York could be at 50N 40W as shown. Then put large circles around the cities between which the airliners are flying.

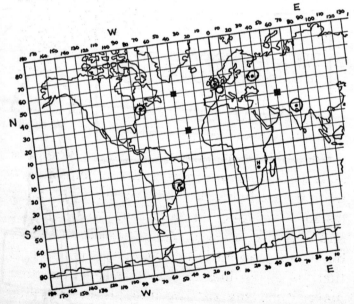

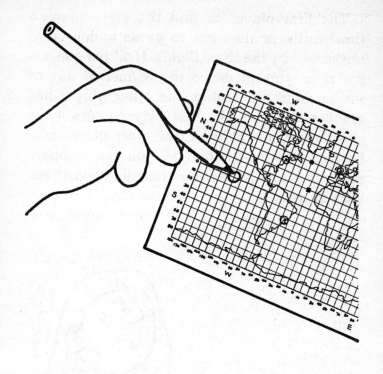

Do not look at each other's map. Now you each have to guess where the other player's airliners are flying. Do this in turn. One player marks a position on their map with a circle and says the position. The other player marks his or her map with a circle in this position. If there is an airliner in this position, the other player must say so. The first player then fills in the circle on the map.

The first player to find the other player's three airliners then has to guess which cities are served by the three flights. If all the guesses are right, this player is the winner. If any of the guesses are wrong, the other player has another go. Then the first player guesses the cities again. In this way, the other player may be able to win. At the end, you can compare each other's maps to check that all the positions were correct.

If you find it hard to play this game, ask an adult to help you with it.

COMPUTERS ON COURSE

Before take-off, the computers on an airliner are given the positions of the two cities and the course to fly between them. The airliner also has devices that measure its movements during the flight. The measurements enable the computers to work out the airliner's position as it flies. If it begins to fly off course, the computers alter the controls to bring the airliner back on course.

To measure its movements, the airliner contains several gyroscopes. These are like toy gyroscopes, and you can use one to see how they work. This activity also needs two people. One person should thread a piece of cotton through the outer ring of a gyroscope and hold it up as shown. Keep the axis of the gyroscope horizontal. Move the hands slowly and see how the gyroscope turns as the cotton turns.

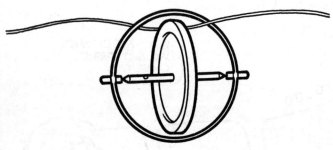

The other person should now set the gyroscope spinning, but try not to break the cotton. Hold

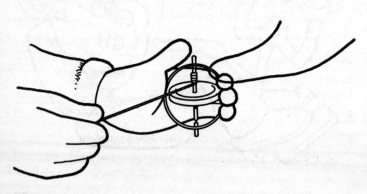

the gyroscope up again, keeping the axis horizontal, and move the hands. This time the gyroscope does not turn. It stays pointing in the same direction.

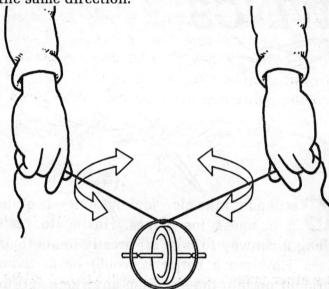

Spinning gyroscopes are suspended in the aircraft so that they always point north–south and east–west, no matter how the airliner moves. Measuring devices connected to the gyroscopes measure the movements of the aircraft around the gyroscopes.

An aircraft may also have other methods of finding its way. It can get radio signals from special radio beacons on the ground below. These guide the aircraft through the air.

CHAPTER 8
WHIRLING WINGS

WHAT A STRANGE WAY TO FLY

*G*etting into the air – and out of it – is quite a business for planes. Having to rush along a runway to take off greatly limits their uses. How much better it would be to zoom straight up into the sky from anywhere and to land anywhere. And it would be wonderful to be able to hover in the air without moving, and to fly backwards if necessary.

We can do all these things in a helicopter. These flying machines with their spinning rotors can fly passengers even to their own doorstep. But helicopters are more than a marvellous means of transport. They can also rescue people from sinking ships and people in trouble on mountains.

RISING ROTOR

A helicopter looks very different to a plane, yet it uses the air to fly in the same way. The long blades of the rotor have an aerofoil shape like wings. A plane has to move through the air for its wings to produce lift. A helicopter whirls its rotor round and round so that the blades cut through the air to produce enough lift to fly. But the helicopter does not have to move to do this. It can therefore rise straight up into the sky.

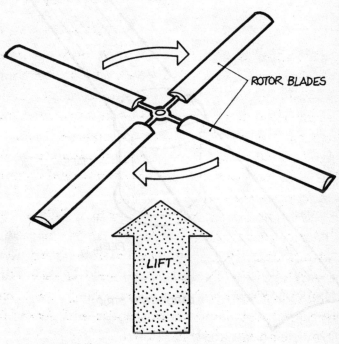

ROTOR BLADES

LIFT

You can show how this happens. Take an empty cotton reel; a light plastic reel is best. Make a pair of rotor blades from firm cardboard. Cut a long thin strip and tape it to the top of the reel as shown. Carefully push a screwdriver through the hole in the reel to make a hole in the centre of the rotor. Now curve the blades as shown so that they have an aerofoil shape.

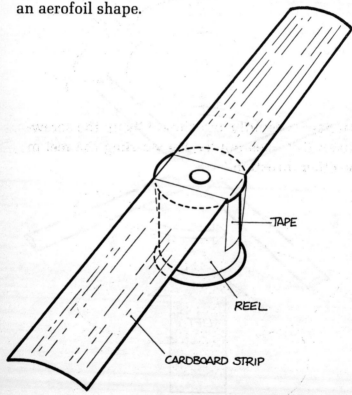

TAPE

REEL

CARDBOARD STRIP

Place the reel on the screwdriver. Wind a piece of string around the reel as you would do with a spinning-top, and pull sharply. The

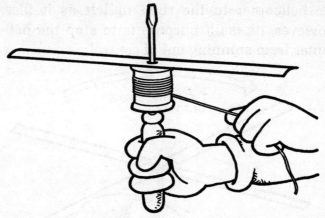

rotor spins rapidly and should fly up the screwdriver. If it does not fly, try whirling the reel in the other direction.

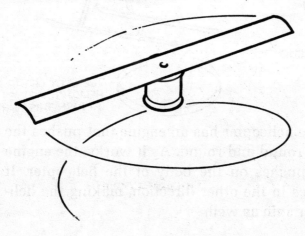

SPIN STOPPER

No helicopter has just one rotor. There is often another small rotor on the tail. This rotor turns the helicopter to the right or left as it flies. However, its main purpose is to stop the helicopter from spinning out of control.

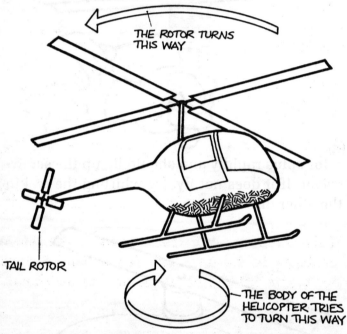

THE ROTOR TURNS THIS WAY

TAIL ROTOR

THE BODY OF THE HELICOPTER TRIES TO TURN THIS WAY

The helicopter has an engine that pushes the rotor round and round. As it works, the engine also pushes on the body of the helicopter. It pushes in the other direction, making the helicopter spin as well.

An activity will show this in action. But do not try to do this activity yourself; it must be done by an adult. Use a large table. Take two round lids and some marbles or ball-bearings.

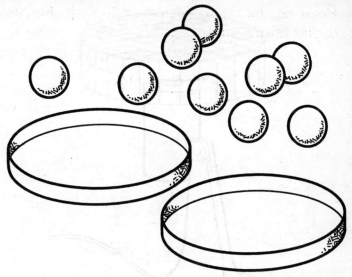

Turn one of the lids upside down in the centre of the table. Place the marbles or ball-bearings in it and put the other lid on top as shown.

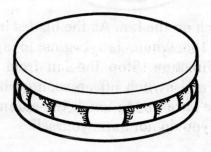

The top lid should spin easily. Place an electric fan on the lid so that the blades will blow air straight up. Make sure the wire is loose so that the fan is free to turn.

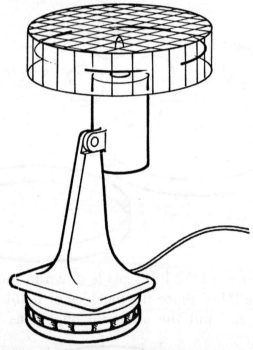

Switch on the fan. As the blades inside whirl round, the whole fan begins to spin in the other direction. Stop the fan from falling off the lid and switch off as soon as it begins to turn. Be sure not to touch the spinning blades so that you do not harm yourself.

As the rotor blades whirl round, the body of the helicopter tries to spin in the other direction. The tail rotor acts like a propeller. It pushes on the tail to stop the helicopter spinning. However, it can change its push so that the tail moves round a little to turn the helicopter as it flies.

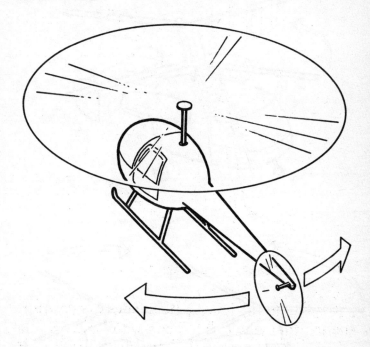

Some helicopters have two main rotors. They whirl in opposite directions so that the helicopter does not spin. Changing the angle of the blades in the rotors makes the helicopter turn.

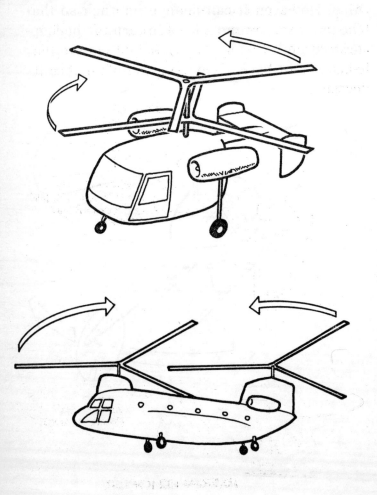

FREEDOM OF THE SKY

How does a helicopter fly so freely through the air? The lift of the main rotor blades overcomes the weight of the helicopter so that it rises into the sky. The pilot can change the angle of the blades in the main rotor. This alters the lift. Making the lift equal to the weight causes the helicopter to hover. Reducing the lift makes it descend.

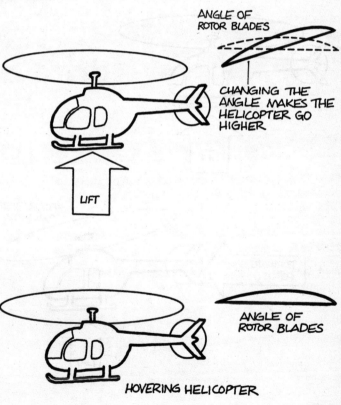

ANGLE OF ROTOR BLADES

CHANGING THE ANGLE MAKES THE HELICOPTER GO HIGHER

LIFT

ANGLE OF ROTOR BLADES

HOVERING HELICOPTER

The main rotor can also move the helicopter forwards, backwards or sideways through the air. This happens because the lift not only forces the rotor upwards. The pilot can control the blades so that the whole rotor tips forwards, backwards or sideways. The lift then also acts to move the helicopter in this direction.

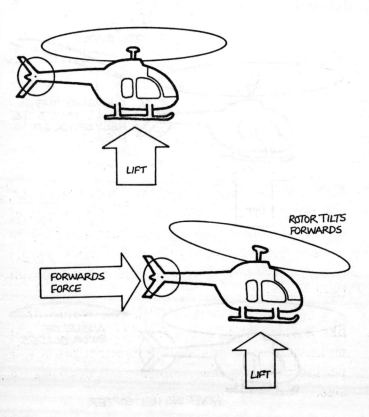

LIFT

ROTOR TILTS
FORWARDS

FORWARDS
FORCE

LIFT

CHAPTER 9
DOWN TO EARTH

*T*here's an old saying that 'what goes up, must come down'. It's true of all kinds of aircraft and their passengers. Normally they go up and come down together. But some people like to jump out of aircraft and come back on their own!

If you tried this (DON'T!), you would drop like a stone. It might seem that the air is not much help in such a situation, but it can lower people safely to the ground. It all depends on size.

MORE SIZE, LESS SPEED

A stiff piece of unfolded paper will show you this. Hold the paper up by the shorter edge as shown and then drop it. It falls quickly to the ground. Do this again, but now hold the paper out flat with two hands and let go. This time it sinks slowly through the air.

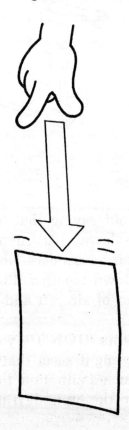

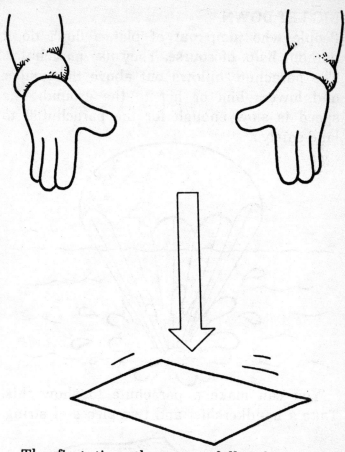

The first time the paper falls, the narrow edge cuts easily through the air. But when the paper is flat, the whole side moves through the air. Because the side is so much larger than the edge, it has to push quite a lot of air aside. This slows the paper down.

BIG LET DOWN

People who jump out of planes don't do it without help, of course. They use parachutes. The parachute billows out above the jumper and lowers him or her to the ground. The speed is slow enough for the parachutist to land safely.

You can make a parachute to show this. Take a handkerchief and two pieces of string.

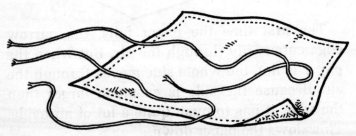

Each piece should be long enough to stretch from one corner of the handkerchief to the opposite corner. Tie the pieces of string to the four corners and knot them in the middle as shown. Fasten a light object like a small reel of tape to the knot; it must not have sharp edges.

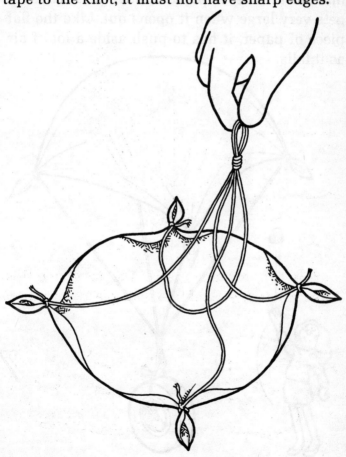

This is the parachute. Take it outside and fold it into a small, neat bundle before throwing it up in the air. Be careful where you throw it! It should open and return slowly to the ground. Air is caught in the parachute so that it stays open as it falls. A parachute works because it gets very large when it opens out. Like the flat piece of paper, it has to push aside a lot of air as it falls.

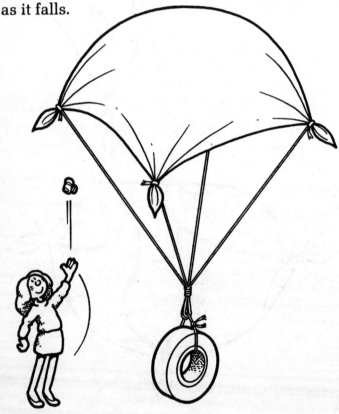

JUMPING FOR JOY

Some fliers carry parachutes for safety, but many people like to jump as a sport. They often use a special parachute called a Ram-Air parachute. This parachute opens out rather like a wing. As the parachutist descends, he or she can move forwards through the air like a glider.

You can make a parachute like this with a sheet of A4 paper and some paper clips.

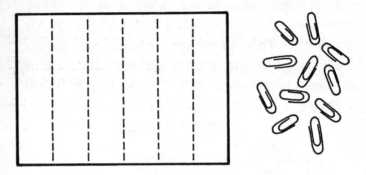

Fold the paper into six strips. Then fasten three clips to the back and two to the front as shown. Next make a chain of six paper clips and attach it to the front two clips. Open out the paper so that the zigzag strips are curved slightly.

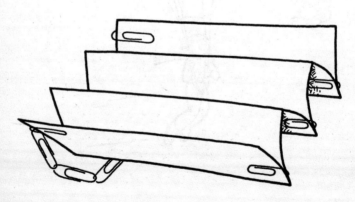

Hold this parachute at the centre and let go. It opens out and then begins to fly forwards as it descends. You may be able to get it to float down some stairs, but do take care doing this.

As the paper falls, the line of clips pulls the paper open and tilts it slightly so that it begins to move forwards. Air moving over the curved surfaces produces a little lift.

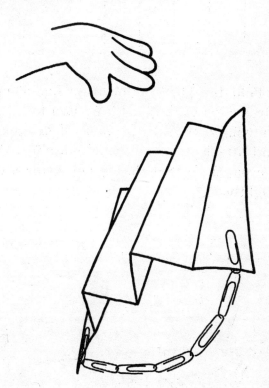

INDEX

Two other Young Puffin Fact Books

EUROPE: UP AND AWAY
Sue Finnie

A lively book packed with information about Western Europe which includes sections on stamps, car numbers and languages as well as topics related to an individual country (from flamenco dancing to frogs' legs).

WATCH OUT: KEEPING SAFE OUTDOORS
Rosie Leyden and Suzanne Ahwai

A book to give children an awareness of the dangers lurking outside on the roads, on their bikes, near water, on building sites, etc. It is full of fun, puzzles and quizzes as well as being packed with information on how to keep safe.

More books in Puffin

PETS FOR KEEPS
Dick King-Smith

A light, amusing book of twelve simple pets, from hamsters to budgies, each with an anecdote and lots of useful and practical hints for pet owners and potential owners. No nonsense, just matter of fact and fun to read.

YOUNG PUFFIN BOOK OF CROSSWORDS
Mavis Cavendish

How do words cross to form crosswords? What are anagrams? Can you fit the letters into the spaces? This is a lively and informal introduction to crosswords, guaranteed to turn you into a fan.

CHECK OUT CHESS
Bob Wade and Ted Nottingham

A basic guide for those learning to play chess. The moves each piece can make are described and there are a variety of exercises to familiarize the reader with them. The principles of checking, castling and so on are clearly explained, as are attacking, defending and the rudiments of tactics.